S T I C K M E N™

The STICKMEN™ Guide to Life

by
Peter Vegas

78 stick-y tips for survival in the 21st Century

CONTENTS

INTRODUCTION

Really good things come in threes. Like the Lord of the Rings films, the Hanson brothers and those Tupperware containers that fit inside each other. But who had any idea the little guys would stick around for a third book?

When it came to the completion of my stick trilogy I really wanted to give you something more. For me, life has changed beyond recognition since my first Stickmen™ book hit the shelves of the world's bookstores, petrol stations and Kate's Key-Cutting and Shoe Repairs in Robertson Mall, Kaiapoi, New Zealand. With this book I wanted to give you a chance to change your life as well.

Over the past ten years there has been a huge boom in the self-help book industry. Why? Do people need more help? Or are there more people who have decided they would like to try to help others? I don't know. I've never read one. Not enough pictures and too much like hard work. I'm Generation X. I have a short attention span and crave instant gratification.

Chicken Soup for the Soul? That sounds OK — if it actually is a soup I can drink that's good for my soul. Although if they want to make it a real hit, how about a chilled chicken soup with extra caffeine and guarana in a can, so I can drink it on the go? But long, boring books? Not my cup of tea. Or soup. Still, there must be something in this self-help stuff so it got me thinking. What if my Stickmen™ had something to say? What if these quiet, simple men, stuck in a very complicated time, had a few words of wisdom they could pass on to you?

Well, it turns out they do.

This, the resultant book, kind of plays out like an extended session at the pub with me — i.e. long, drawn-out periods of mindless, seemingly irrelevant dribble punctuated by fleeting moments of razor-sharp, insightful observation, mostly lifted from other people. But if you can find a few little gems in here that make sense to you — ideas you can take away and use — that will make me happier than when I get on my private Lear jet 'Stick One' and discover that the on-board DVD library has been stocked with the latest episodes of American Chopper.

So, dive in. I've cleverly broken the book up into sections. Self-help experts tell me this gives the reader the feeling that there is a series of layers to the help being offered. On one layer you'll find lessons about perseverance, while other layers talk about having a plan, sticking to the truth and learning from experience. Dig right down and you'll get to the layer on lessons from history.

I loved history at school. It was always in the afternoon and my seat was at the back of the class. When the sun came streaming in, it was easy to drift off to sleep. I was going to say the rest is history but of course I didn't sleep all of the time; sometimes I was awake and then I'd draw Stickmen™ to pass the time. Isn't it interesting that years later these two loves have been brought back together like some kind of trippy high-school history department reunion to which only Stickmen have been invited?

You will also find a guide to drawing your own Stickmen™ — and Stickwomen. That's right, I want to empower you to create your own ideas. The pen, pencil, crayon, paintbrush or burnt stick is in your hand. Use it. Who knows, if there is a Book 4 I might need your help filling it.

For now, my job is done. My Stickmen™ have spoken. Their words of wisdom await you. And remember, 'Sticks and stones can break your bones. But sticks in pics can really help you.'

Cheers,

Peter Vegas

Stickman rising from the primordial ooze.

1. In the beginning.

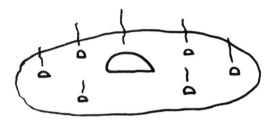

2. A little bit later

The First STICKMAN™

What are the origins of the Stickman™? Did he evolve out of the primordial ooze? Some would have you believe he was created when a collection of sticks just fell randomly. But what are the odds? And how do you explain the head? I've never seen a stick bend round into a circle naturally. No, I believe there is more behind the perfect stick form. I think he was created by a higher power. Probably using a pen or pencil. And I reckon that this higher power was probably left-handed and it happened on a Thursday.

Tip #1

Nobody's perfect.
Funny head
One arm is short
Crotch is weird
Foot is wonky

Tip #3

Make big plans

Tip #4

Stick it out.
Why did you take your legs off?
Because I'm not going anywhere

Tip #5

Be happy. If you can't, get help.
This Stickman is on Prozac.

Tip # 6

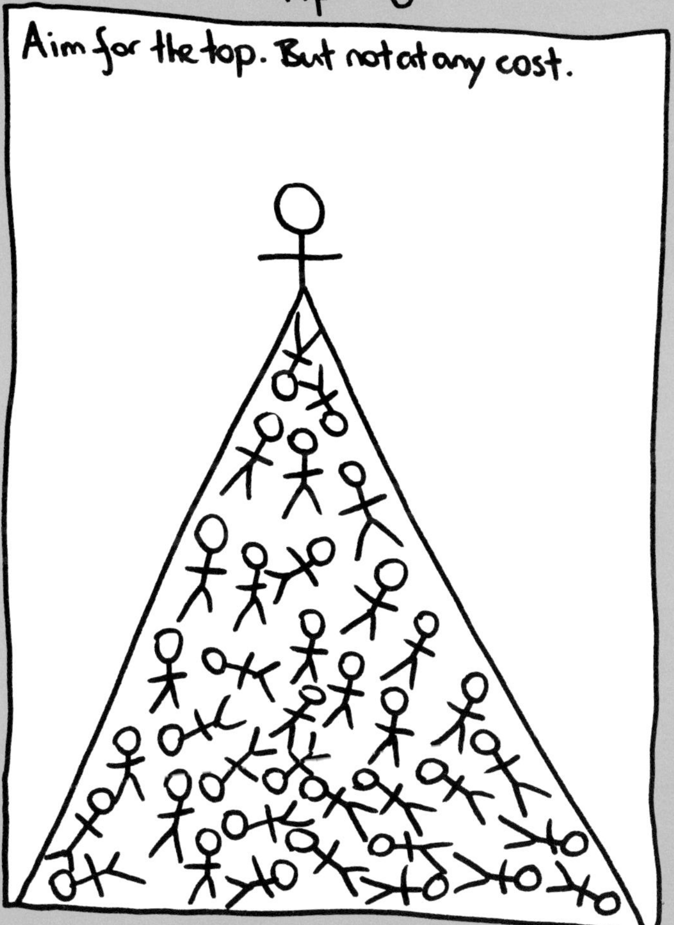

Tip # 8

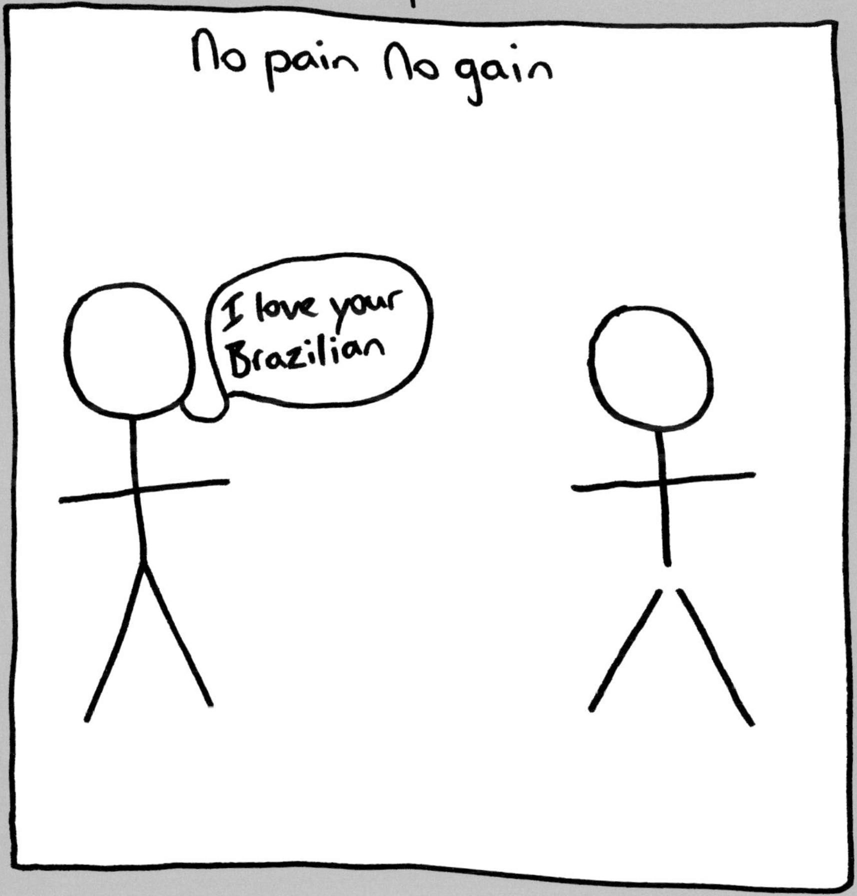

Tip #10

Don't give up coffee.
No one likes a quitter.
How you feeling?
Just Grande thanks

Tip #11

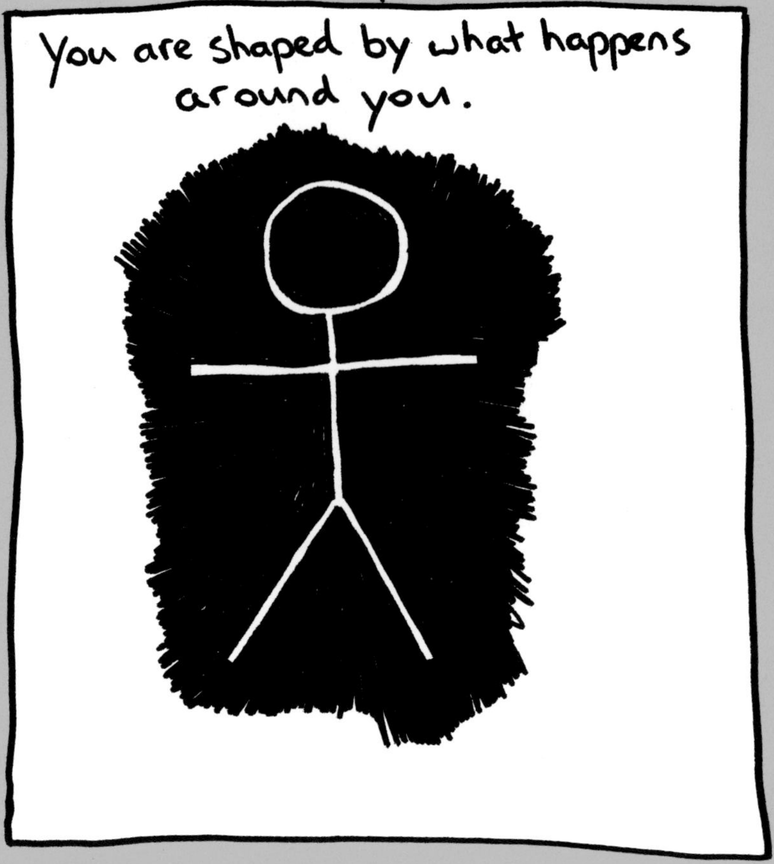

Tip #14

When you lose don't lose the lesson.

Tip #15

Tip #16

Look for the good in everything.
Like the snooze button on an
alarm clock.

Tip #17

Share your problems. If no one will listen, use money.
Just lie back on the couch.

Tip #18

Tip #21

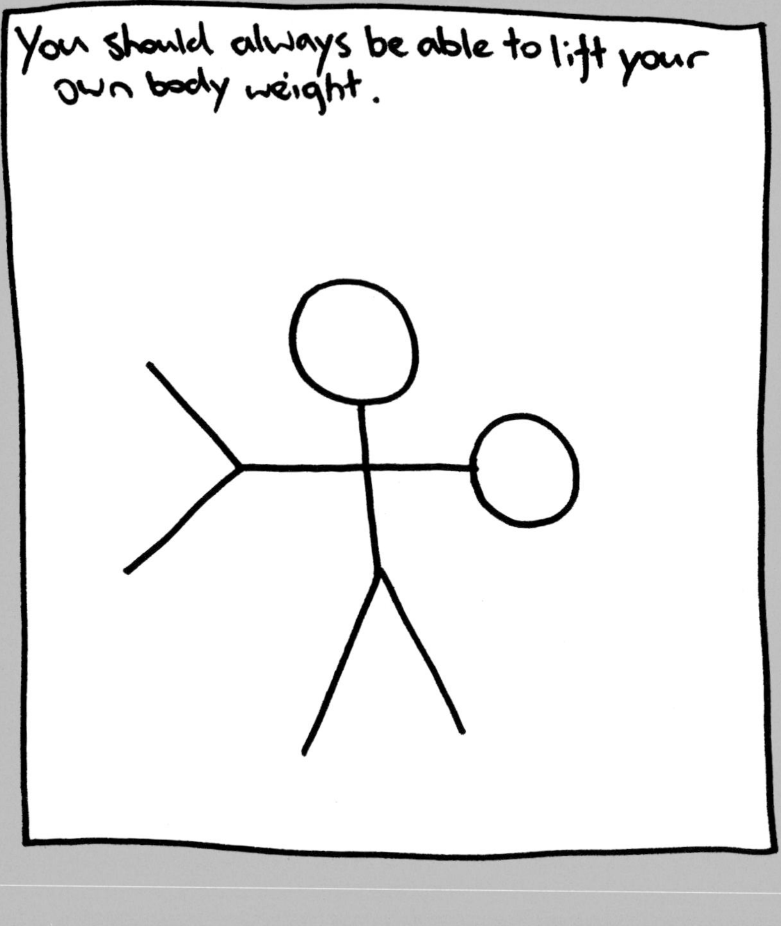

Share your knowledge.

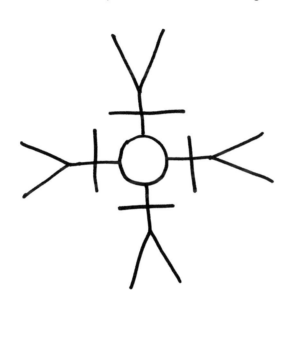

Tip #23

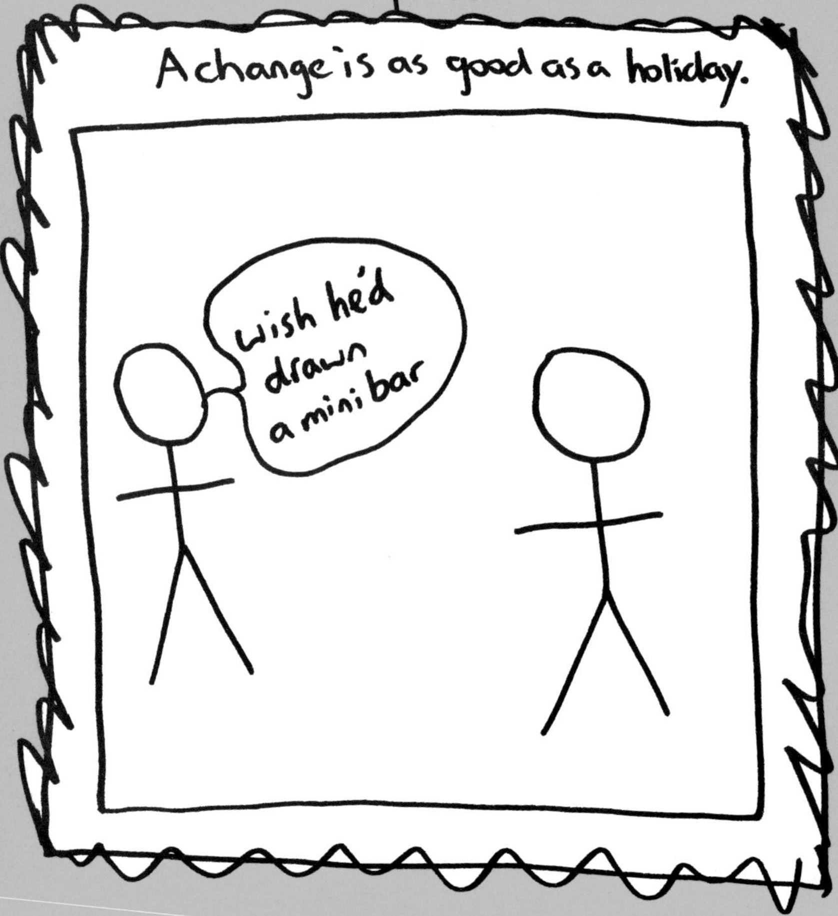

Tip #24

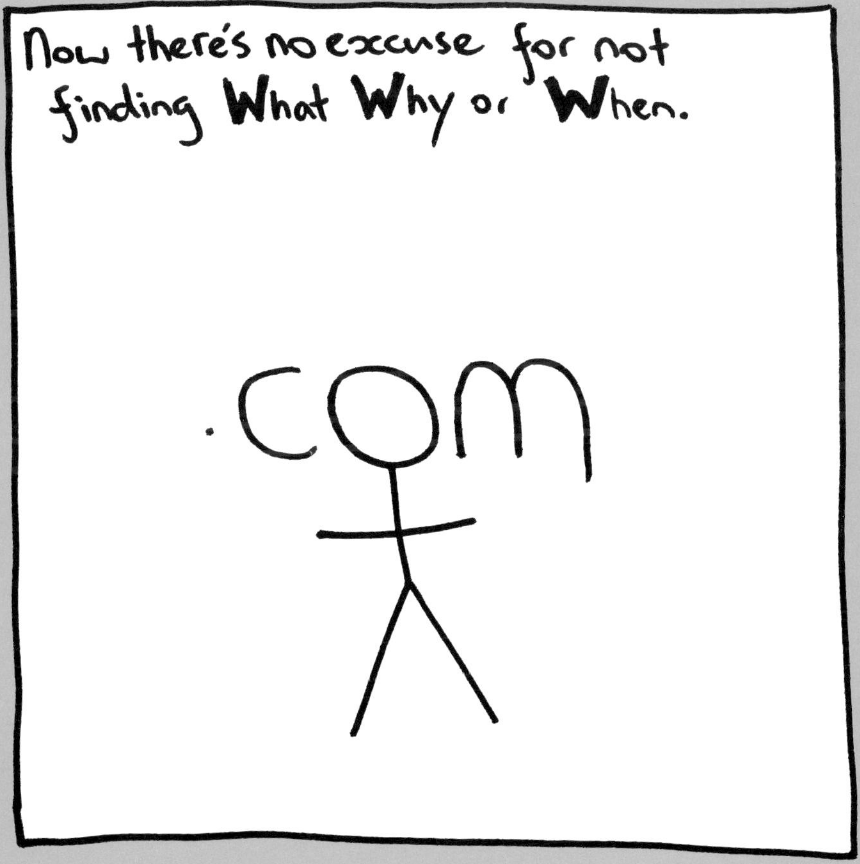

Tip #26

Stick

to a

Plan.

Tip #28

Go to University.*

*I don't really think it's that important to get a degree but i liked this idea.

Tip #30

The only shoes you should be trying to fill are your own.

Yoga works.

Tip #35

They say the pen is mightier than the sword. Use both.

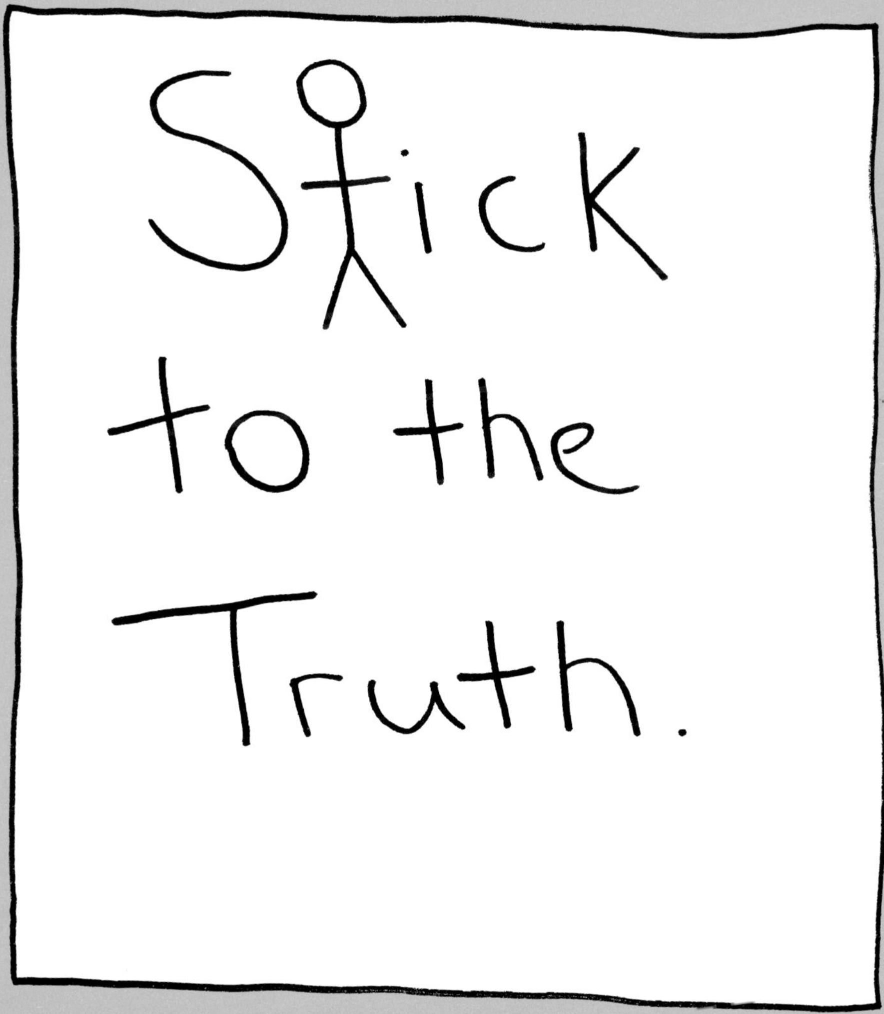
Stick to the Truth.

Tip #37

Men really do only have one thing on their minds.
Hi. I thought I would swim over and introduce myself.

Tip #40

From far away everyone looks the same.

Tip #41

Tip #42

Don't mistake monotony for Deja Vu.

Tip #43

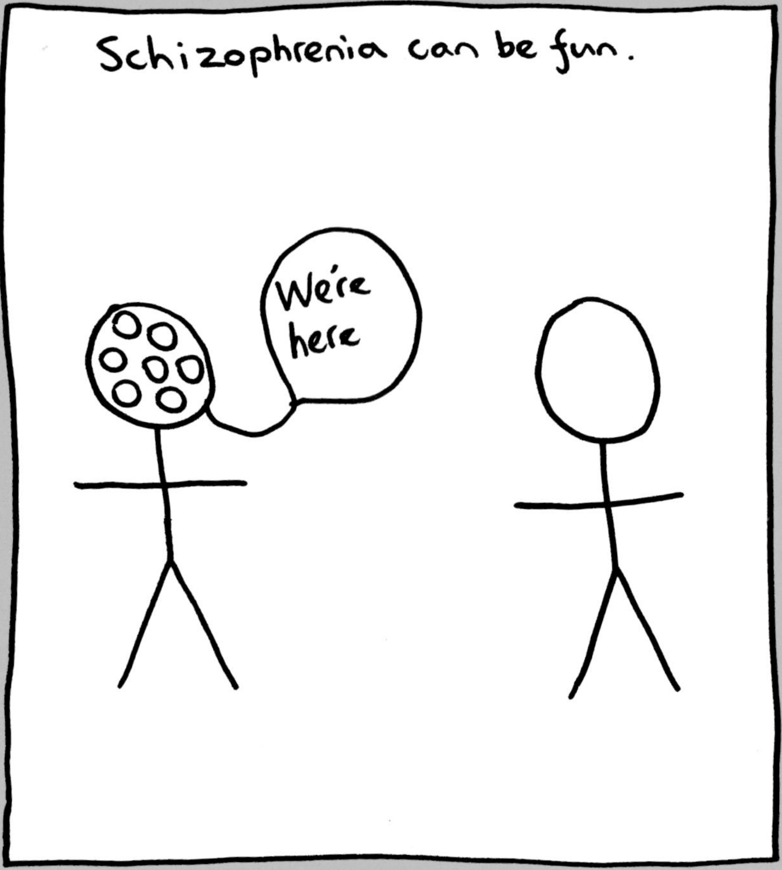

Tip #44

Computer games will do your head in.

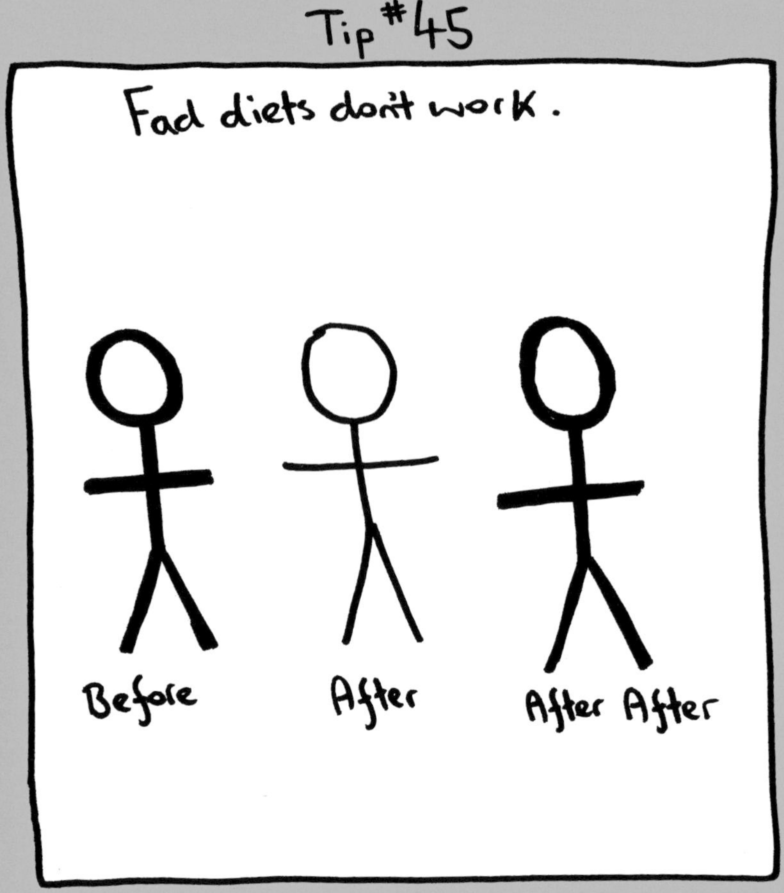
Tip #45
Fad diets don't work.
Before
After
After After

Tip #46

Drunk people look stupid.

Tip #47

The problem with trying to see the world in black and white is you end up looking stupid.

Tip #48

Be tolerant of other people's cultures.

Tip #50

Where some see a mistake others see a success.
For example. Do you see a badly drawn Stickman or John Hurt in his brilliant role as the Elephant Man in the 1980 film?

Tip #51

There are two types of people in this world.
One are the type who think there are only two types of people in the world.
I'm us. You must be them.
and then....

Tip #52

There's everyone else.
open minded people
not
cagey people
Bad people
clever people

Tip #54

Stickmen and stones can break your bones. But a stickman with a gun will do some real damage.

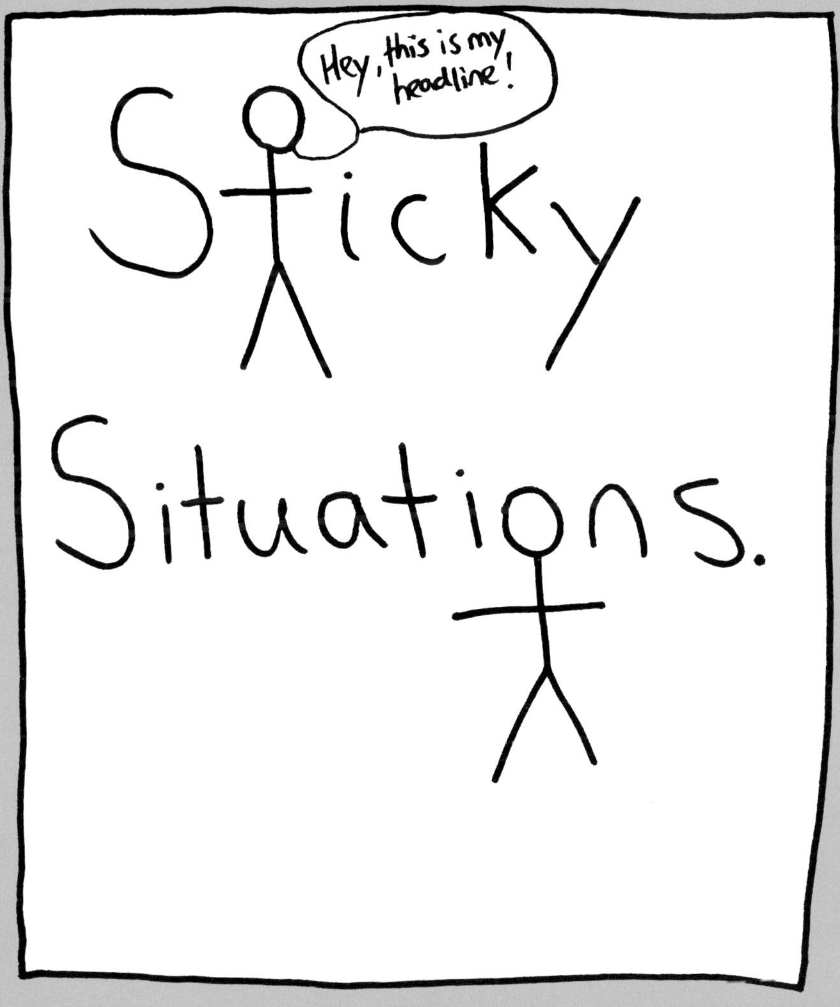
Hey, this is my headline!
Sticky
Situations.

Love triangles get messy.

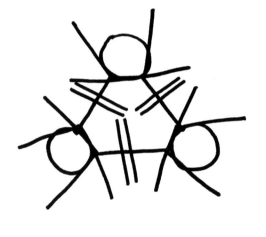

Tip #60

Sometimes the only thing blocking your path is you.

Tip #62

Global warming is a fact.
Have fun while you still can.

Sticksnowman

Tip #63

There will always be louder and more aggressive persons than yourself.
1 2 3 4 5 6 7 8 9 10 11
Are you listening to me?
I said hit me!

Tip #64

Men are from Mars, women are from Venus.
What planet are you from?
the little red one.

Tip #66

Just because someone will take your money to do it, doesn't mean you should.

Tip #68

You always have choices.
I need you to work late again.
I can't. My goldfish died today and we're holding a funeral in my bathroom tonight.
I need to look for a new job.
get stuffed!

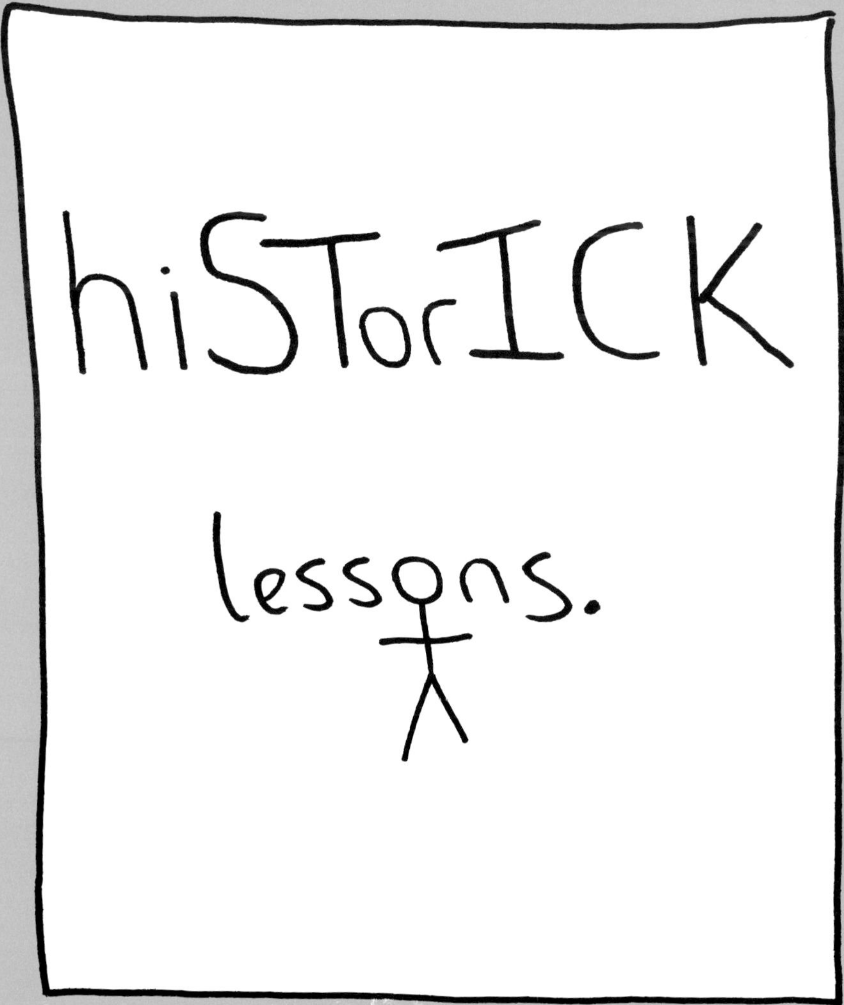
hiSTorICK
lessons.

Tip #70

Simple and genius have alot in common.

Tip #71

One man's terrorist is another man's freedom fighter.

Tip #73

Don't believe everything the men in charge tell you.
you're wrong Galileo

Tip #75

Every great idea was thought up by someone like you.
you
the inventor of the wheel
Thomas Edison
That guy who thought up the internet

The
Sticky
End.

What are you doing with the
box you live in?

Don't feel trapped.

Invite someone to share your box.

Be creative

You can make it fancy.

Use your life to make your box
into whatever you want....

Because, when it's all said and done
we all end up in the same box.

The End .

DIY Stickmen™

You know when you flick through a book and think 'I could have done that.' That's how i felt about War & Peace. Incredible as it might seem a few people felt the same way about Stickmen™ 1 + 2.

So here's your chance to have a go. Don't worry, I won't throw you in the deep end. Here are some directions for all you budding stickmen™ creators.

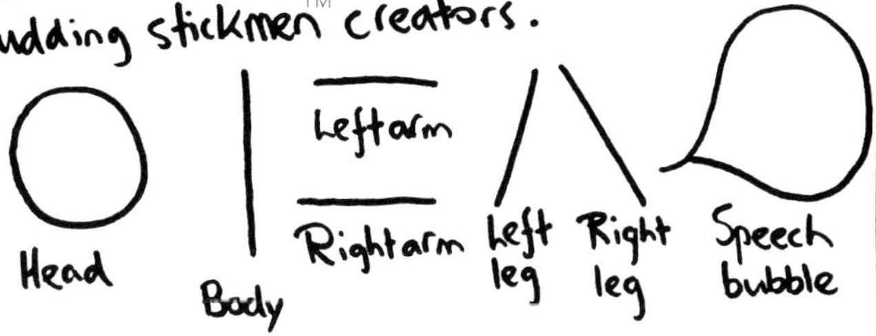

Head

Body

Leftarm

Rightarm

Left leg

Right leg

Speech bubble

Now use the next page to create your own stickman™ idea.

Your idea here ↑
If it's any good send it to me so i can use it
in my next book.